CONTENTS

To Patricia and Desmond Lavelle

PART I   FROM 1700 TO TWO MILLION YEARS AGO

In our search for Ireland's earliest landscape we must go back to the beginning
of the earth's history. I do not propose to look into 'Black Holes' or to take
shelter from the 'Big Bang', but will start at the point where we find Ireland's
oldest rock, on which we can walk about. I hope to bring a group of ambulant
naturalists with me on a geological walk down the Irish corridor of time, a walk
that will occupy at least 1700 million years. To keep us lightly equipped, I must
assume that at all times there will be no difficulty in breathing, and that our
clothing need not be more varied than what would be available today for
visiting various parts of the earth's surface. Thus we avoid the necessity to lug
along breathing-apparatuses to enable us to survive until the atmosphere reaches
today's proportions, and fire-resistant clothing to wear until the earth's surface
cools down to bearable conditions. But we shall have a magic carpet at hand to
whisk us from one part of Ireland to another. The carpet will carry an inflatable
boat and scuba-diving equipment.

Legend tells of seven-league boots, but we are more interested in relative
year lengths. The members of the party must be experienced naturalists, and
twenty-five will be the minimum age. Our route will be strenuous at times, and
beyond the physical capacity of anyone over sixty-five. So we have forty
walking years at our disposal. If we are to get any impression of change around
us as we walk along, at the start of our journey the years by which we record our
age will have to be of the order of forty million times as long as today's years,
when we come to the Ice Age they will be fifty thousand times as long, and
during the post-glacial period they will be two hundred and fifty times as long.

Plate tectonics; mountain-building; glaciation
Our first rendezvous is on the tiny island of Inishtrahull, 8km (5 miles) north-
west of the Inishowen Coast in Donegal (see 1.1). As we assemble we cower
behind a rock about 1700 million years old, the oldest rock so far recognised in
Ireland. There we take shelter as geological forces, of a strength unimaginable
today, rage around us. Rock-rafts of continental size, or plates as we call them,
are already adrift on the earth's surface. If two rafts collided, an edge could
either be forced upwards, creating mountain ranges, or downwards, creating an

5

1.1. We look down on our starting-point, Inishtrahull, as the magic carpet takes off. The rocks are about 1700 million years old, and their disturbed nature can be seen clearly; a fault cuts diagonally across the bottom of the picture. (Cambridge University Collection of Air Photographs)

oceanic deep. These processes are called plate tectonics. Sometimes plate margins fractured into small pieces, as in a jig-saw puzzle, which went their own way. Inishtrahull is such a piece. It bears no relation to the nearby much younger rocks in Donegal or Derry. It could fit against the Hebrides or Greenland. During such movements gigantic volcanoes were also active. Many already existing rocks, if they were not remelted, were metamorphosed into new rock types; the rock against which we are leaning was so altered. We shall see many examples of the effects of these great early forces as we walk around Ireland.

The plates move relatively slowly, but geological time has been long enough for them to cover enormous distances across the surface of the globe (see 1.2).

6

The plate carrying Inishtrahull was then towards the bottom of the globe, in the southern hemisphere at about the level of South Africa. The poles of the earth were already sufficiently cool for ice-caps to form there, and for glacial deposits to be formed in high latitudes. If we move to north-west Ireland, while many

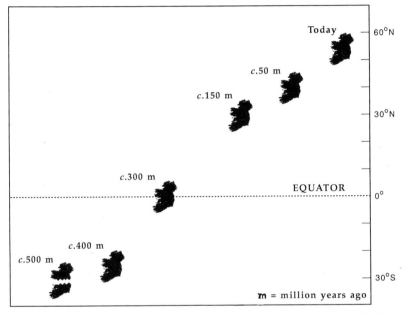

1.2. *Before 500 million years ago, Ireland was in two parts, separated by an early Atlantic Ocean, but this ended when the American and the European plates moved together to form a great Euro-American plate. The two parts of Ireland were welded together along a line running from Clogherhead (north of Drogheda) to Galway Bay. The united plate then lay in southern latitudes, at about the level of South Africa, and during the succeeding 400 million years Ireland was carried slowly northwards for a distance of about 9000km to reach its present position.* (Redrawn by Matthew Stout, after J P B Lovell.)

millions of years elapse around us, we can see in several places typical glacial deposits, formed about 500 million years ago. But this ice came from Antarctica, not from the North Pole we know today, the source of our much more recent ice-sheets.

Life on the sea-shore
Time is rolling steadily on, and we are now 600 million years from the present day and have moved to Leinster. In the oceans life-forms are developing in myriads of different ways, and we can find fossils of only a few of these in Ireland.

7

In imagination, our party is standing on the top of Howth Head, on the north shore of Dublin Bay. In reality, we cannot be standing there because at the time of our visit the area is covered by sea, on whose floor clays and banks of sand are being deposited. By later earth upheavals these loose deposits have been metamorphosed into slate and quartzite, on which we take up our position.

If we look towards the south we see the knobby top of Bray Head and the conical outlines of the two Sugarloaf mountains. Quartzite is resistant to erosion, and these resistant knobs were formed from once sea-floor sands; their surrounding slates form lower ground.

A brief digression. If we turn back the clock by a mere 150 years from today, and have powerful binoculars at hand, we can see a figure bending over the slates at the foot of Bray Head and scanning them closely. The figure is Thomas Oldham, of the Geological Survey (see 1.3), and he is looking in a puzzled manner at small fan-like impressions in the slates, impressions that repeat themselves over and over again (see 1.4). Slowly he is forced to accept that they cannot be entirely fortuitous, but must be the fossil impressions of some form of life. If so, they must be older than those then known from other parts of the earth. Are they animal or vegetable? He pondered long over this, and eight years later showed them to the scientific world, which acclaimed them as *Oldhamia antiqua*.

1.3. Thomas Oldham, Professor of Geology, Trinity College Dublin 1845–50.

We look north from Howth Head, towards the conspicuous Lambay Island. At the time of our visit, now 450 million years ago, the area is still below the sea, but in those waters many more new forms of life have appeared. In the rocks at Lambay and on the adjoining coast at Portrane we can find fossils from quite a range of animals. A little further north lies the village of Skerries, which takes its Scandinavian name from the small islets off the coast here. Here the rocks are again fossiliferous, but slightly younger in age.

Today it is impossible to see just where the margins of these early seas were, but our party finds them quite easily, and as we walk the shore at low tide we spot tossed-up trilobites, jointed animals with hard outer coats like the modern beetle, brachiopods, with paired calcareous shells like the modern 'cockle and mussel', and graptolites, thin rods carrying many little cups, without close parallels in the modern seas, but perhaps related to the corals. If our stroll lasted for several million years we might start to find scraps of strange fish on the beach, because the vertebrate world was now struggling to come into existence. But there were many predators around, and these first fish were armoured with heavy bony plates, the ancestors of the modern fish-scale. We venture into our scuba-suits, and are delighted to see a wide range of animals (see 1.5). On the slopes above the beach our botanists find their first land-plants — primitive forms perhaps related to the modern horse-tails. Seaweeds have a much longer history; they were distributed worldwide long before we set out from Inishtrahull.

1.4. Oldhamia antiqua. *These frond-like fossil impressions, about 550 million years old, were discovered some 150 years ago at Bray, Co Wicklow, by Thomas Oldham. At the time, they were the oldest fossils known to exist.* (J Joly)

1.5. In our scuba-suits, some 430 million years ago, we stare at the plates of coral on the sea-floor, and at the stalked sea-lilies (Crinoids) swaying gently in the currents. A relative of the octopus swims past. (Natural History Museum, London)

9

If we move further north and follow the strand beyond Clogher Head in Co Louth, we notice some new forms among the shells. Similar forms occur in North America and Sweden. The Iapetus Ocean which separated the North American and European landmasses was then wide enough to have different faunas on its opposite shores, and these were brought into confrontation when plate movement, about 400 million years ago, crushed the two shores together and obliterated the open water. The line of collision can be traced across Ireland, and by this movement two separate landmasses were united into an early Ireland.

The first 'Emerald Isle'; primitive land-plants; freshwater fish
The closure of the Iapetus Ocean was the first scene in an enormous, lengthy geological drama in which the North American and the European plates were crushed more and more closely together. Our starting-point, Inishtrahull, is a small piece of early rock that was once attached to Scotland or Greenland. We can picture it as a raft that floated on the earth-moving waves, and so rode out the worst of the renewed upheavals. We return there, and take refuge for many millions of years. The crushing movement resulted in an enormous arc of mountains and valleys, generally called the Caledonides, which can be followed through Scandinavia, east Greenland, Scotland, north-west Ireland, Newfoundland and the Appalachians. Gradually the movements died away, and 350 million years ago we land in Donegal, and climb the hill just south-east of the Visitor Centre at the Glenveagh National Park. Today we would only be 400m (1312 ft) above sea-level, but then we would have been very much higher, because hundreds of metres of rock have since been stripped away by erosion. From our rather risky perch we watch the quartzite peaks of Errigal and Muckish take their shape, as the softer rocks around them crumble away. Ireland is now in the latitude of Brazil, and the climate is hot and wet.

Mountain torrents are coursing down around us, and they carry off the eroded debris to spread it out over much of Ireland as great sheets of sand and gravel, which occasionally hold transient freshwater lakes. Some debris goes as far as the open sea just south of Ireland. The loose sands and gravels were later cemented into sandstones and conglomerates. These rocks can still be seen in many parts of Ireland, where they are known as Old Red Sandstone.

10

We make our way inland, to Knocktopher in central Kilkenny, as there is a lake not far away at Kiltorcan. As we approach we see that the lake is surrounded by trees, but on nearer inspection we discover that they have neither cones nor seeds, but reproduce from spores, like the modern fern. Searching still more closely we find one form that does produce primitive seeds. In the shallow waters at the lake-edge we are amazed to see a large freshwater mussel, whose descendant, the Swan Mussel (*Anodonta cygnaea*), still lives in some Irish lakes. There are also giant crustaceans, vaguely like the modern lobster. We have our boat, and a net appears from nowhere. We do catch a few fish, and although they have a primitive appearance we can see in their bony skeletons many resemblances to those of modern fish.

Although we are very exited by our discoveries, our ears gradually pick up a distant rumble, which can only arise from the breaking waves of an approaching sea. We retire immediately to the high ground of the Wicklow Mountains. These hills are largely composed of the igneous rock, granite, which was injected from below during the Caledonide mountain-building era. The erosion we have already seen in Donegal exposed the granite, but left it at a height above that of the oncoming sea. Ireland has now crept up to the level of the Equator, and the water is warm, like that of the Caribbean today.

At first the water was shallow and clear, and was inhabited by a wide range of invertebrate animals, which built up exoskeletons of calcite ($CaCO_3$). Corals abounded, and occasional reefs broke the surface of the sea. We get our boat and go scuba-diving, to find them just as rich in life as the Great Barrier Reef is today.

When these animals died, immense quantities of calcite debris accumulated on the sea-floor. This debris was gradually lithified into limestone, and despite later disturbance and erosion this limestone occurs to the present day over about two-thirds of Ireland's rock-mantle.

The sea slowly shallowed into tropical swamps, and these were invaded by giant trees, descendants of the forms we saw at Kiltorcan. Masses of decaying vegetation accumulated (Pl 1), and as millions of years went by, the debris was gradually compressed into coal. The first air-breathing amphibians are beginning to appear, and we make our way to Castlecomer in Kilkenny where these animals are common both in the water and on the banks of a winding

11

a)

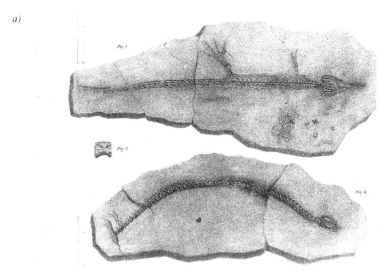

b)

1.6. a) Some 450 million years ago, vertebrate forms were developing, and these amphibian fossils from the Kilkenny lagoon clearly have backbones and limbs.
b) Early terrestrial reptiles. (Natural History Museum, London)

channel in a swamp; there are also early lizard-like reptiles (see 1.6). For the first time on our trip the entomological members can unfurl their nets, for there are plenty of spiders and dragon-flies in the forest.

Later geological developments compressed the plant debris of the swamp-

12

forests into seams of coal, which had great economic value, especially after the nineteenth-century Industrial Revolution. Geologists created the name 'Carboniferous' for coal-bearing rocks, but this name now covers the whole cycle just described, both inundation leading to limestone, and shallowing leading to coal. So Ireland's most abundant limestone is Carboniferous limestone.

A west-European upheaval; mountains of south-west Ireland; deserts return

About 300 million years ago there was vigorous movement between the European and the African plates. The Harz Mountains in central Germany give their name to the ranges of mountains that were erected, the Hercynides. A great thrusting movement pushed north into Ireland, culminating in the rising of the mountains of Kerry and Tipperary, as the Carboniferous rocks and the Old Red Sandstone were crumpled into east-west folds. North of the Galty Mountains in Tipperary (Pl 2) the forces were less, and if we take our stand in the Clare hills just north of the city of Limerick, to watch the spectacular rise of Galtymore, we ourselves will only be carried gently upwards as the ground under our feet rises to a modest degree in response to the pressures.

Ireland now finds itself in the northern hemisphere, at about the latitude of Egypt today, with a desert climate. Most of the country is above sea-level and large quantities of red desert sands are being set free by erosion. Occasionally local depression allows an arm of the sea to be formed, but the connection is rarely long-lasting, and rock-salt and gypsum (the sulphate of calcium) are deposited as the briny water evaporates away.

These shallow lakes, known as lagoons, are chiefly in north-east Ireland, and to give ourselves a vantage-point we move on to the upper slopes of the Sperrins in Co Tyrone. Where Carrickfergus is today, on the northern edge of Belfast Lough, we see the last remnant of a lagoon whose underlying deposits are rich in beds of rock-salt. There was a similar lagoon at Kingscourt in Co Cavan, from whose waters gypsum was deposited. The modern plasterboard factory there utilises these deposits.

We now have to move about with more care, like modern big-game hunters, for we are entering into the age of the dinosaurs. These reptiles, which are often

13

of enormous size, are to be found in all habitats, earth, water and sky, where they will flourish for about one hundred million years. Their remains are almost non-existent in Ireland, but 225 million years ago we make a pilgrimage to the Newtownards area of Co Tyrone, where a small reptile, crossing the muddy edge of a pond, has left a trail of his foot-prints, each about 7cm (3 ins) long.

By and large the topographical features of modern Ireland bear the imprint they were given by the Hercynide mountain-building forces of long ago. Since then there have been minor vertical movements, but the thrust of the last 200 million years has been erosion, not deposition. We think of the Kerry mountains as impressive, but they are only the cut-down ghosts of ranges of Alpine proportions that once existed there.

Although mainland Ireland largely stood above sea-level, it was surrounded by basins in which sediments were deposited, and it is in these basins that the modern search for gas and oil goes on — a search that has added enormously to our knowledge of the geology of Ireland's setting.

America and Europe part company; chalk-seas cover Ireland; vigorous volcanic activity in the north-east

Great changes for our party are now on the way because about 180 million years ago a north-south split appeared in the great Euramerican plate, a split that was to widen and widen until the modern Atlantic Ocean was created. That widening still continues, though at a slow rate today. In these movements Ireland drifted back towards the Equator, and became largely flooded by the sea as sea-floor upheaval brought about a worldwide rise in sea-level. Our party has again to scramble up the slopes of the Sperrins, if we wish to keep our feet dry. We can now botanise fairly safely, because the dinosaurs are on the point of extinction. And there is much to excite us because modern-looking flowering trees and shrubs cover the landscape.

The sea is warm and its waters are calcareous, and in its upper layers algae, which secrete small units of solid calcium carbonate, are blooming. A layer of chalk-mud is accumulating on its floor, often to a considerable thickness. Then suddenly our wanderers notice that the tide has turned, and the chalk-mud, now compacted into a weak rock, chalk, is being exposed and immediately attacked by erosion. In north-east Ireland some chalk will survive because later lava

14

flows protected it. Elsewhere, only a few tiny surviving patches, one near Killarney, Co Kerry, suggest that chalk probably did once cover most of the Ireland we know today.

We stay in the Sperrins, but by the time we have come to within sixty-five million years of the present day we have to brace ourselves against further geological perils. If our nerves hold we shall have a ringside view of the volcanoes (Pl 3) and lava flows that raged for some fifteen million years in north-east Ireland. To these activities we owe the modern Giant's Causeway, Fair Head and Slemish Mountain in Co Antrim, the central core of a now-vanished volcano. Further to the south-east, the igneous structures of the Mountains of Mourne are being created.

The first lavas poured out before the surrounding chalk had been eroded away, and our botanists examine the very limy soils that had formed on the chalk and the plants they support. They give a rousing Three Cheers, because for the first time they recognise some of the trees — pine, cypress, monkey-puzzle, alder — that still grow in the modern world. Sometimes long intervals separated the flows, long enough to allow plant-supporting soils to form on the surface of the lava, and our botanists are kept busy examining the successive stands of woodland.

Even after the lava flows have ceased, there is further cause for alarm when, about thirty-five million years ago, a large block of rock, only some 40km (25 miles) east of where we stand, begins to subside; as it does the diverted rivers pour water into the basin, which becomes the first Lough Neagh. The slopes around the lake remain wooded, and some members of the party think they have suddenly been transported far westwards, as they see redwoods, swamp-cypresses and black gums, trees now confined to North America, growing all around them. Their debris remains as thick seams of lignite scattered through the clays and sands.

We meet this kind of woodland everywhere in Ireland, and the lignitic deposits that formed from its vegetable debris must have been widespread. But subsequent erosion — and from now on the geological story is largely one of erosion — has reduced them to tiny surviving pockets here and there.

To get an impression of this erosion we turn our steps to Fermanagh, Leitrim and east Galway. Everywhere the once widespread chalk has vanished, and the

15

1.7. The Burren, Co Clare, some ten million years ago. For a very long time the rocks of Ireland have been wasting away due to continual attack by weathering. Carboniferous limestone dissolves in rain, and its surface is dissected into pinnacles and ravines. Here one of our party inspects the fretted surface of the Burren. Today's surface is very different, as it has been planed flat by later ice-sheets.
(A J Sutcliffe)

deposits of Carboniferous coal that underlay it are also gone, except from the higher ground around Lough Allen in Leitrim, where thin seams of coal project from the hill-slopes. We are surrounded by wide expanses of karstic limestone, characterised by deep sinkholes and dissected here and there into upstanding cliffs, all wasting away under the solutional powers of the rain (see 1.7). We cross over into the Marble Arch area of Fermanagh, where the surface we are walking on is many hundred of metres above the present surface. From far below we can hear the rushing waters of underground streams flowing in large solution channels. Since we heard those streams, the land-surface has dropped dramatically, the water-table has dropped also, and our solution-channel has become a spectacular cave, which attracts thousands of visitors each year.

But the story of erosion is a puzzling one. We move on to a point near Headford in Galway. Here in a hollow in the limestone there is a small deposit of lignite, which the local farmer uses for fuel. The plants of the lignite are the same as those at Lough Neagh, and our party scratch their heads as they ask 'How can this lignite, thirty-five million years old, still be preserved here at modern ground-level, when elsewhere the same period of time has eroded away many hundred metres of rock?'.

Modern temperatures set in; erosion continues apace
About twenty-five million years ago, Ireland has reached its present position on the surface of the globe, and is now moving away from North America at a very

slow rate. Our party begins to note that the nights are getting chilly, and summer heats are no longer those they have become accustomed to. The fall in temperature is irregular, periods of lowering being followed by periods of recovery, but always with a downward trend.

If, about thirteen million years ago, the party decides to make a side-trip to northern regions, they will find polar ice-caps beginning to form. Unlike the previous changes of temperature our party had experienced as they moved up and down the globe on their Irish raft, this change of temperature appears to have been climatic in origin, and worldwide in extent.

During an upbeat phase, when temperatures were slightly higher and seasonally more uniform than today, we make our way to Hollymount, just north of Carlow town, to see a fine stand of woodland with strong North American overtones. Among the conifers are pine, redwood, hemlock and umbrella pine, and of the deciduous trees we see alder, birch, hazel, holly, hornbeam and willow; some palms are also scattered around. The soil is fairly acid, as the ground flora includes heather and rhododendron, and also the moss, *Sphagnum*, so common in Irish bogs today.

Since our visit, continuing erosion has brought about chemical alteration in the surrounding limestone, and created a vertical pipe filled to a considerable depth with altered rock of smaller volume. Downward collapse has thus taken place, and some forest debris, now altered to lignite, has also moved down. Today, if we visit the site with a drilling-rig, we can get samples of the lignite for detailed study. Such solution-pipes are widely scattered through the limestone in Ireland and are often very deep; some have been drilled to a depth of more than 150m (492 ft) without reaching solid rock.

We have come to the end of this first leg of our journey, the finishing-tape clearly labelled 'Only two more million years to go'. Our course so far has been sometimes like a Monte Carlo Rally, as we racketed along bumpy tracks through menacing ravines, with volcanic bombs whirling overhead, sometimes like a luxury cruise on tropical seas whose islands are covered by palms. We see a building labelled 'De-briefing Headquarters', and thankfully slip through its doors for a relaxing hot bath, and a stiff drink.

17

PART II   FROM TWO MILLION TO 10,500 YEARS AGO

Across the road from where we stand there is a similar building, but it is labelled 'Briefing Station', and there some shocks await us. The first is our new watch, set to a time-unit with years fifty thousand times as long as those of today. There will be no problems with breathing, for the atmosphere will be the same as the present day. We will not be venturing into tropical parts, but we will want clothing that will protect us from icy blasts. Our magic carpet will be there to assist us when necessary.

It is explained to us that in East Africa there is a gorge, the Olduvai Gorge, and that the earliest firmly dated substantial remains of man, *Homo sapiens*, have been found exposed in its cliffed sides, and are dated to 1.7 million years ago. If we regard man as an important feature of the last great unit into which geological time has been divided, the Quaternary, then the second phase of our walk must begin here. For simplicity, I have rounded the date off to two million years.

Alternating cycles of heat and cold; changing woodlands
In the late nineteenth century it was agreed, after much controversy, that there had been a Great Ice Age, a time when the ice-masses on the earth's surface had expanded enormously. At first only one advance was admitted, and the Monoglacialist School reigned. But by the 1920s it had been demonstrated that at least in the Austrian Alps there had been four glacial stages of advance, separated by stages of retreat. Today, aided by many discoveries made possible by the development of new sophisticated techniques, workers in this field are coming round to the view that at least during the last half million years, there have been alternating phases of heat and cold. The basic rhythm of the cycle seems to be about 100,000 years, though there are divergences, and the cycle is not symmetrical as the cold takes a long time to build up, while the subsequent recovery to warmth is relatively short.

We take our places on the magic carpet, and have not proceeded very far before we run into fog. Someone in the party has a volume of poetry in his knapsack, and he gives us an appropriate reading from Coleridge's *Ancient Mariner*.

18

And now there came both mist and snow,
And it grew wondrous cold:
And ice, mast-high, came floating by,
As green as emerald.

And through the drifts the snowy clifts
Did send a dismal sheen;
Nor shapes of men or beasts we ken —
The ice was all between.

The ice was here, the ice was there,
The ice was all around:
It creak'd and growl'd, and roar'd and howl'd,
Like noises in a swound!

The fog will persist as our carpet speeds on for at least 1.5 million years. At times hoar frost will appear on our eyebrows, and we will know that Ireland below is in the grip of a cold phase. At other times the fog will be more like a sea mist, and we will feel clammy and sweaty, knowing that Ireland is enjoying a climate at least as mild as that of today.

Suddenly, about 450,000 years ago, the fog clears, and we see woodland below. Our carpet quickly sets us down in a clearance at Ballyline in Co Kilkenny, not far south of Castlecomer. Our first glimpse makes us feel at home, for we see oak, elm, alder and yew. But we also see fir, spruce and hornbeam, trees not native in Ireland after the end of the Ice Age, but which grow well today when planted in forests and demesnes. There is another tree, the wingnut (*Pterocarya*), a stranger in western Europe today, though some forms of it still survive in Turkey. One treeman recalls that we have seen this tree before, in the forests that surrounded Lough Neagh many millions of years ago. There the wingnut had for companions few trees of modern Ireland, but was surrounded by redwoods and cypresses, trees today confined to North America. Those Lough Neagh forests held many exotic forms, but they were picked off one by one by the ensuing phases of cold. The wingnut managed to stagger as far as Ballyline.

We remount our carpet and so re-encounter thick fog. But if at Ballyline we got only a snapshot of one stage of forest, we shall do better on our next *19* descent, for we shall be on the ground for many thousands of years, and can watch the landscape of Ireland change as various stages of woodland succeed one another.

We land near Gort in Co Galway as the last wisps of fog are clearing away, perhaps about 350,000 years ago. The previous cold stage is just ending, and willows are beginning to invade open country where herbs and juniper predominate. Birches and pines then create the first woodlands as trees begin to return to Ireland from the south. High forest is established when oak, ash, elm, hazel and yew, laced with plenty of ivy, appear. But there is no hornbeam. This is much the picture we would have in Ireland today if man had not removed so much of our woodlands.

Large mammals were common in western Europe at this time, and we keep a keen eye out for elephants, rhinoceroses, horses and bison. But if they are there they elude us, and though we inspect many ponds, we never see the beaver or the pond tortoise. These animals were preyed on by palaeolithic hunters, who were quite widely distributed in Britain; no trace of either animals or hunters has yet been found in Ireland.

But now the excitement of our party rises to fever point, because for several thousands of years immediately ahead of us we shall be moving on into what Ireland's modern woodlands would have developed into if they had remained undisturbed. The climate of this warm stage reaches its acme, and slowly begins to decline. The soils are becoming less fertile, and greedy trees, like the elm, can no longer compete. Large conifers, the fir and the spruce, move in. Deterioration of climate and soil continues, and bogs begin to form. With them rhododendron appears; we have rhododendron in Ireland today, but it was introduced by nurserymen in the eighteenth century. Escaping from gardens, it has flourished wherever soils are acid, and become a pest in woodlands, such as the forests around Killarney. Our botanists are delighted to see several unusual heathers, varieties that today have their headquarters in the Cantabrian Mountains in Spain. There are also other heathers that no longer grow in Ireland.

But our all too familiar fogs begin to swirl around us once more, and tantalisingly prevent us from seeing the closed vegetation in which we have been wandering gradually break up into open tundra, which in turn becomes covered by ice and snow. Most reluctantly, we take our seats on the magic carpet once more.

On again, at first through freezing fog, but as we pass the 200,000-year mark, we come to a patch of warm mist. We feel in our bones that a warm stage, with Ireland smothered in woodland, must lie below us. But our carpet has developed a technical fault and refuses to descend. And so an opportunity to clear up one mystery is lost. From today's point of view, when we know so little detail of the climatic oscillations that we believe have a cycle of 100,000 years, we cannot be sure at what peak to place the older warm stages. Was the Gortian Warm Stage really at 350,000 years, or are we hovering over it now? Somewhere there must be a cycle, of which as yet we have not been able to find any fossil record.

We move on, and after another 100,000 years we begin to feel that warming again. But now a new problem. Our carpet cannot find any place in Ireland to land, and we are diverted to Stansted, north of London. There to our agreeable surprise we find ourselves exploring a low-lying landscape with wandering river channels. As with the Gortian, our arrival has been timed well, for the early birchwoods are replacing the tundra from the final phase of the preceding cold stage. In turn the birch is invaded by the pine. We watch as these early woods develop into closed forest with elm, oak, hazel, alder and maple. We are now truly in a warm stage, for the summer temperatures in which we are basking are 2°C higher than our summer temperatures today.

If our wanderings were to take us past the site of Trafalgar Square, we would have to keep a keen watch-out, as there are lions on the prowl. We would also give a wide berth to wandering elephants. There are ponds around, and in these rhinoceroses and hippopotamuses are wallowing. If we go to College Green in Dublin, will we see them there? Man was not common in Britain at this time, and we are not likely to meet any cousins.

Looking more closely at the woods in some areas we see a broad-leaved tree, which at first sight looks like a beech, but closer examination shows that it is a hornbeam (a tree not native in Ireland today). We watch as hornbeam expands in the woods, and some spruce appears. We are very privileged to have seen these woodlands, for the next expansion of ice will sweep away the trees and plough up the muds in the river channels. If we move north in England we may find in the deposits laid down by that ice, blocks and lumps of mud whose fossil content tells us that these hornbeam woods once stretched still further north. Such lumps of mud are our only proof that these temperate woodlands once existed in Ireland also.

21

So we remount our carpet and over-advance our watches to allow us to return to Ireland and pay a sneak visit to the modern Wexford coast to see a lump of this hornbeam mud embedded in glacial deposits that have not yet been formed. We come down on the beach at Blackwater, not far north of Wexford town. Here a keen-eyed glacial geologist noticed among all the cobbles of glacial gravel one different lump, about the size of a cricket-ball. Cutting it open, he discovered it was of tough, dried-out mud. He brought it to a pollen specialist, who instantly recognised from its diagnostic pollen content of hornbeam and spruce that it must have been dragged up by later ice from a woodland channel somewhere to the north of Wexford. This is our only evidence that, like East Anglia, Ireland 150,000 years ago enjoyed a warm stage, when temperatures were slightly warmer than they are today.

We put the carpet into reverse, go back 100,000 years, and are ready for new adventures. As soon as the now familiar fog appears again, we know what we are in for. But this time it is a short haul, for we soon come down on the north shore of Tralee Bay, not far from Fenit. Cooling has not yet proceeded very far, and here at Kilfenora we are in open woodland, where pines are scattered through grasses and sedges. There are also occasional alder, hazel, holly and oak, but no spruce or hornbeam. We take samples of the peat, which in the laboratory is shown to contain traces of radioactive material; when the ratio of thorium to uranium has been determined, it indicates that the peat has an age between 115,000 and 120,000 years. There must have been either a very slow onset of cold and these trees were the survivors from earlier more dense woods, or else after the establishment of real cold and the extinction of trees, the climate ameliorated for a short period, making possible the development of scanty tree-growth.

We are now firmly on the ground, and thanks to the Kilfenora peat we have obtained our first chronological 'fix'. We are *en route* for the acme of a cold stage, and we watch with fascination as a new panorama unfolds around us. The last of the Kilfenora shrubs give way to open tundra (Pl 4). Snow-beds, where the winter snow fails to melt the following summer, appear and steadily increase in size. On higher ground the snow-beds coalesce into solid ice, and this begins to creep down to lower levels. Ice begins to form here too, and gradually rises into a massive dome. Under the weight of the overlying ice, the basal ice becomes plastic and begins to flow radially outwards. We must either mount the ice or retreat in front of its advance. Though we cannot observe it, once a certain volume of ice has accumulated, its weight becomes sufficient to depress that part of the crust of the earth on which it rests.

A temporary retreat; temperatures rise

The development of ice in Ireland perhaps reached its maximum extent about 75,000 years ago, when almost the whole of the island was buried by ice. The upper slopes of the mountains of south-west Ireland probably remained uncovered, and roped together we make a perilous ascent of Mount Brandon in Kerry, across snow-banks and small glaciers. We choose Brandon because here the ice meets the sea and becomes water-born until its thinning edge breaks up into icebergs.

One night we hear the trickling sound of running water, and we realise that melting is beginning to overtake freezing; are we really starting on the last leg of our icy journey? This will be the most interesting part of our trip because the ice, though basically on the retreat, will still from time to time launch counter-attacks. But being on a smaller scale they will not create such havoc among earlier deposits, and so leave us some evidence of the warmer conditions that led to the ice retreat.

A trek along wet, thinning ice brings us to the east shore of Lough Neagh to Aghnadarragh, in Co Antrim, about 50,000 years ago. Temperatures are rising rapidly. The ice thins away and gravels appear, and a sparse scattering of tundra develops. In places streams are cutting channels in the gravels, and there are sudden whoops of delight as our geologists see projecting tusks and molar teeth of the woolly mammoth; but there is no trace of the animals themselves. We so concentrate on this that for some time we fail to notice thin forest springing up around us. There is open woodland dominated by spruce, pine and birch, but there are also other trees scattered around, like hazel and yew. Our coleopterists find plenty of beetles (and we all find mosquitoes). There is general agreement that conditions around us are like those in central Scandinavia today. But we soon notice that it is getting chillier, the trees fade away, tundra expands, and ice creeps upon us once more.

We keep ourselves warm by indulging in semantic argument. A glacial stage

23

is a time of maintained severe cold, a stadial is a short cold period, an interglacial stage is a warm period sufficiently genial and prolonged for forest of modern European type to establish itself (Gort was clearly such an interglacial stage), an interstadial is a phase of modest warmth, too cool or too short for high forest to expand. What is the status of Aghnadarragh? My view is that it is an interglacial because of the presence of the warmth-demanding hazel and yew, but I am out-voted, and it is ruled to be an interstadial.

The ice that re-expanded over Aghnadarragh certainly got south of Lough Erne in Fermanagh, but as we approach that area it thins again, and at Hollymount, near Lisnaskea, north of the upper lake, we see tundra re-appear about 40,000 years ago. Taller plants endeavour to gain a foothold, and dwarf birches and willows and some heathers begin to establish themselves among the grasses and sedges. The insects in the ponds confirm our feeling that the temperature is about that of northern Scandinavia today. But the phase of amelioration is short, snow-beds appear, ice re-expands. Clearly this was an interstadial.

Woolly mammoth and other animals; permafrost and pingos

In this area the ice-margin must have fluctuated considerably, for our next stop will be at Derryvree, also not far from Lisnaskea. But before we reach that point, we will have crossed an important threshold. We have carried along with us throughout our trip a radio-electric clock, powered by gamma rays emitted from dying atoms of radiocarbon. Unfortunately our clock can only start to work when the impulses rise above a certain level, a level that was reached about 40,000 years ago. A point of red light appears on the clock, and we know we are in business. At Hollymount we failed to get any reading, but here at Derryvree the clock tells us that we are still 35,000 years from home.

The scenario at Derryvree is by now familiar. Frozen soil appears, and as soon as it has thawed some growth of grasses, mosses, a few flowering plants and scattered juniper bushes are visible, and also a flourishing of vicious mosquitoes. This is all the evidence that a later advance of ice has left us at Derryvree. But if we move south to the Blackwater Valley in Co Waterford, we can carry the story further. Here copses of birch and willow are scattered through rich grasslands, giving sufficient food for large grazing mammals. We

24

only saw the bones of the woolly mammoth (see 2.1) at
Aghnadarragh in Antrim; here we see them grazing lazily,
accompanied by wild horses, Irish giant deer and reindeer.
But there is no sign of the woolly rhinoceros that we saw a
long time back in East Anglia. Skulking around we see packs
of hyenas dragging carcases into their cave-dens.

In a strong come-back, about 25,000 years ago, the ice
now expands again (see 2.2). We mount the magic carpet to
take a quick run along its southern margin. We start just west
of the Saltee Islands in Wexford, turn the corner at Carnsore

2.1. Woolly mammoth, Les Combarelles,
France. This sketch could have been drawn
by one of our party near Dungarvan, Co
Waterford, 35,000 years ago. (After Breuil)

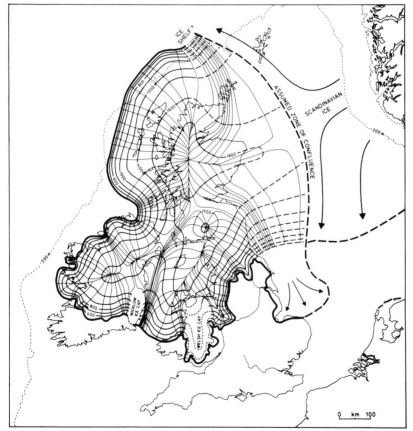

2.2. A contoured map of the ice-mass that largely covered the British Isles, perhaps 25,000
years ago. (Oxford University Press.)

25

Point, and follow the western edge of a great ice-lobe that fills the basin of the Irish Sea. It presses against the slopes of the Wicklow Mountains but does not override them. The edge makes a hair-pin bend south of Dublin, and sweeps down the west side of the mountains as far as Leighlinbridge in Carlow. From our carpet we can see that there is a small independent ice-mass on the top of the mountains. We turn west and head for the Shannon Estuary, where the ice-edge runs out to sea. Our carpet now climbs higher, and we can see that the mountains of Cork and Kerry also have a private ice-cap. South of the ice-limit the mean annual temperature is around 0°C, and as the unprotected ground radiates away its contained heat, the ground below us is freezing to greater and greater depth. These are permafrost conditions, such as cover vast areas of Alaska, arctic Canada and north Siberia.

In summer the surface of the permafrost will melt to a depth of some metres, creating an active layer, the former soil being now a mixture of sand and stones with a porridgy consistency. Convection currents gradually set up a slow circulation in the sludgy mixture. Just as cooling has produced hexagonal columns in the basalt of the Giant's Causeway in Co Antrim, the rising currents in the sludge adjust themselves in the same way, with a polygonal network of erect stones delimiting the columns. In winter we take a stroll across the glacial deposits of south Wexford, re-frozen by winter cold, and observe the patterned ground formed by summer melting.

Remaining in Co Wexford, we move on to Tinnacarrick, 5km (3 miles) south-east of New Ross. We climb the rocky knoll, which rises to a height of 80m (262 ft) above the surrounding glacial deposits that lap against its lower slopes. It is autumn, and winter frosts are closing in. Summer heat has created an active layer, but there is still frost below, and water cannot escape downwards. As we watch, the surface of the active layer freezes, leaving unfrozen material in between two frozen watertight layers. If the slope is at a low angle, not too steep, but also not too flat, then ground-water will feed itself into the still unfrozen material. But increasing winter cold ensures that a point will come when the water in the unfrozen material must also freeze, expanding as it does so. The weakest point is the frozen crust of the active layer, and as we watch, a giant blister slowly arches up the crust to form what Eskimos, who are familiar with this feature, call a pingo.

We survive the winter, huddled together on the top of Tinnacarrick, and eagerly await the spring. The thin layer of sand and stone perched on top of the ice lens is the first to thaw, and it slides down the flanks of the lens, to accumulate as a raised ring around it. The lens melts next, and as it has lost material to the surrounding ring, it leaves a hollow behind it. Pingos formed very freely in the Tinnacarrick area, and if we walk there today we see the characteristic form of the fossil pingo, a depression surrounded by a raised rim (see 2.3). The rim shows that it is a pingo, not a place where a dead ice lump has melted, leaving a hollow without an enclosing rim.

2.3. This collapsing pingo in Canada is similar to what we saw when we looked down from a hilltop in Wexford. The ice-core of the pingo is melting, and soon only a raised rim of earth surrounding a hollow will remain. The polygonal pattern of surface-cracks shows that the ground is still frozen. (T L Péwé)

We summon the magic carpet and again retrace the ice-limit from Wexford to the Shannon. To the north on our right we have the ice-sheet that will shortly begin to melt away, exposing irregular morainic mounds of sand and gravel. To the south on our left the surface of the ground is locked in permafrost, which on melting will reveal patterned ground and pingo, which can be followed all the way from Wexford town to Castlemaine in Kerry. Subsequent cold phases in Ireland do not seem to have been severe enough to create permafrost on this scale.

Kettle-holes; eskers; drumlins

The thaw we observed from Tinnacarrick was the first sign of renewed amelioration, and we know that soon the ice-edge will begin to fall back. We move to just north of the town of Kildare, where three rocky knobs, known as nunataks — the Chair of Kildare, Dunmurry Hill and Grange Hill — are just beginning to emerge through the thinning ice. Some members of the party get out their geological hammers and start looking for fossils, because the rocks

27

2.4. (Opposite)
The gravels and
sands of eskers are
built up inside
tunnels in the ice.
When the ice melts
away, high-standing
esker ridges appear,
as can be seen in this
Icelandic ice sheet.
(R J Price)

here contain the remains of the same sort of animals that we saw alive on the sea-shore near Clogher Head in Louth about 400 million years back.

The main ice lies to the north-west, in Counties Longford and Roscommon, and from there enormous quantities of meltwater are being discharged. Great masses of sand and gravel are being swept across the low ground where Kildare stands today. The meltwaters ebb away or change direction, and the sands and gravels come to rest in a large plain, which today we know as The Curragh, whose well-drained level surface makes it an ideal site for racecourses and military barracks. Occasionally large lumps of ice were carried along, and left buried in gravel. When the final melt-out took place, the water from the lumps drained away through the gravels, the gravel above the ice subsided, and a series of hollows, or kettle-holes, were formed. Today small ponds often occupy the hollows.

After a long period of retreat, the ice began to expand once more, but it failed to reach its previous limit. In the Irish Sea it came to a halt about 17,000 years ago near Clogher Head in Louth; it split against the Hill of Tara, and from there its boundary ran south-west as far as the mouth of the Shannon, where its limit perhaps crossed the older moraine. On this occasion the melting-away is very rapid, and we watch as great quantities of water carrying gravel and sand discharge themselves from exit-tunnels at the base of the ice. If the main volume of meltwater changes course, then the slackening streams will fill up the abandoned channels with sand and gravel. If we sit around for a few years and watch the ice decay, then the silted-up tunnels will appear as sinuous ridges of sand and gravel, which today we know as eskers (see 2.4).

But our party has one great disappointment; they do not succeed in witnessing the birth of a drumlin, and so clearing up one of the great mysteries of glacial studies. Drumlins, small aligned oval hills of glacial material, stretch in a wide belt across north-central Ireland, from Down to Mayo (Pl 5).

We move up into central Mayo, to the vicinity of Castlebar. The ice is already very thin, and we can see the tops of drumlins protruding through it, packed like eggs on an egg-merchant's tray. It is clear that they have been moulded sub-glacially. Just as today's glaciologists do, we scratch our heads and ask 'Were they extruded in this form from the base of the moving ice, just as a butterfly may lay a sheet of oval eggs on the surface of a leaf? Could we not

28

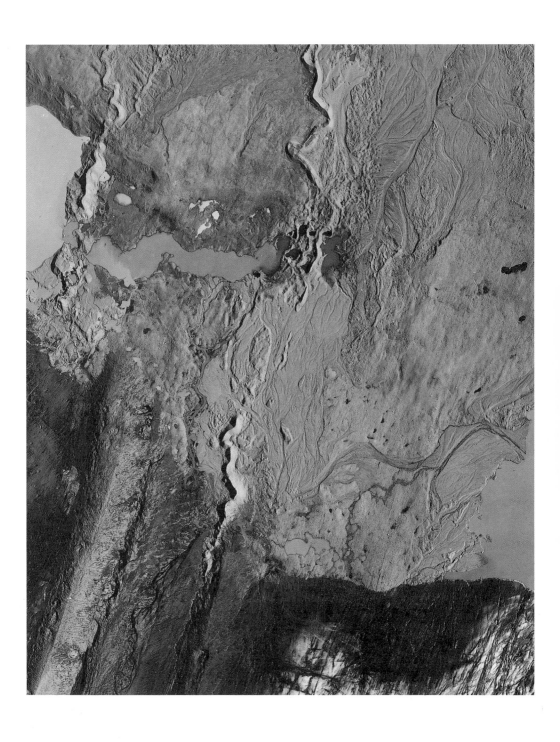

invent some type of submarine that could drill a channel for itself through the ice?' We would be able to sit inside the submarine and examine the contact between the ice and the embryonic drumlin.

Still puzzled, we move on to Clew Bay, off the Mayo coast, where rising waves are beginning to cut sections in the coastal drumlins. Some of these show that the bases of the drumlins are of stratified sand and gravel laid down in water, but they also show that, in the same way as a tortoise has a dome-like protecting carapace, many of the drumlins have a capping of glacial material, apparently plastered on by moving ice. Fierce arguments break out, but no conclusions are reached as to how both deposition and cutting away have resulted in the typical drumlin form.

We get out our thermometers as temperatures continue to rise to values at least as high as those of today, and perhaps a little higher. We move to Ballybetagh, 15km (9 miles) south of Dublin, and our watches say 12,000 years ago. Rich meadows, with juniper and a few birches, spring up around us, and to our amazement we see a party of live Irish giant deer grazing in a nearby hollow. A sheltered valley here was especially favoured by the deer, and as we wander on we get occasional glimpses of reindeer also. We take soil samples, because the young soil is probably very rich in as yet unleached mineral nutrients. Thus the grassland may be more nutritious than modern grasslands, and this could explain how the Irish giant deer could afford to discard his large antlers each autumn, and to grow them again, still bigger in size, the following spring.

Surely we must be at the end of this leg of our journey. But 'No'; a nip returns to the air and we reach for our heavier clothing. We hear of icebergs off Slyne Head in Galway, and we stand there and watch them stream past, propelled by a current of Arctic water. Coastal Europe freezes under its influence. In Ireland the grasslands break up into tundra; snow-beds appear and grow in size; glaciers form in the mountain valleys. We visit Glendasan, near Glendalough, Co Wicklow, and see, not the modern ESB power-station, but a tongue of ice pushing down the valley (Pls 6 & 7). Our watches say 11,000 years ago. But this cold-snap does not last long, and the glacial part of our trip does end 10,500 years ago, when temperatures are the same as today.

30

PART III FROM 10,500 YEARS AGO TO THE PRESENT DAY

We again visit the briefing-station to adjust to our new time-scale and to contemplate the next stage of our journey. One year of our normal life-time will equal 250 years as we move along. We see no need to anticipate geological hazards, climatic extremes or great distances, but we will require invisible cloaks. We will pass by many human groups at various stages of technological development, but all bound together by beliefs, which take many different forms, in supernatural forces, which must be either venerated or appeased. Elaborate ritual will play an important part in the lives of many of the groups, and we would not wish these to be interrupted by our appearance. Nor do we wish to be physically attacked as potentially hostile invaders.

Land-bridges attract new animal and plant life
As soon as cold water no longer reached the Irish coasts, temperatures bounded up and the recolonisation of the land by plants and animals began in earnest. Land-bridges linked Britain to the continent and Ireland to Britain, and the western shore of Europe formed an approach-road to the bridges.

At this point I must confess that I take a strong personal view on the dates to which these land-bridges survived, a view that many of our party do not share. At least two very complex factors are involved. When ice forms on a global scale, much water is extracted from the sea, whose level falls; such movement is called eustatic. As ice forms on land, it places a local load on the earth's crust. We picture an isolated circular ice-mass, gradually increasing in size and weight. As it presses down, crustal matter must be displaced, and this rises as a peripheral rim or bulge some distance ahead of the boundary of the ice-mass. Such equalising movements are termed isostatic. As long as the ice-mass continues to grow, the rim advances and grows higher. When the ice-mass wanes, the rim retreats and sinks. Thus the land is moving isostatically, and basic sea-level is moving eustatically, and so a complicated series of shore-lines at different levels will be recorded in coastal beaches.

During the last cold stage an enormous ice-mass formed in Scotland, and the peripheral bulge lay to the south of Ireland. The Irish Sea emerged as a parallel-sided canal, and as the bulge retreated up the canal it lifted the canal-floor up

Pl 1. (Opposite)
(See p11)
Castlecomer, Co
Kilkenny. Here, about
250 million years
ago, we wander at the
edge of a wooded
tropical lagoon.
These trees are long
extinct now, but we
still burn their debris
in our fires. There
was plenty of volcanic
activity in the
Limerick area about
this time. (From Life
Before Man by Spinar
and Burian, 1972)

above contemporary sea-level to form a bridge. It was a very peculiar bridge because it was not only moving northwards but was also falling in level until it ultimately subsided below the waters of the North Channel, leaving Ireland isolated as an island. Its movement was slow, because soils had to have time to form on it if it was to provide a suitable avenue for immigration. We have sound proof that it survived until at least 7750 years ago, but when the final link was cut we do not know. So for the first stage of our walk, we are constantly meeting new forms of animal and plant life. After that date we rarely meet newcomers, other than those introduced by man.

As we set out 10,000 years ago, we leave behind a barren landscape with few, if any, forms of life. We first cross the open northern grasslands with docks and meadowsweet that we have already seen several times. If we move towards the west coast the grasslands give way to crowberry heaths. Juniper then flourishes for a short period, until it gets crowded out by birches, willows, poplars and bird cherry, as woodland establishes itself for the first time.

Hazel then appears with a rush, and by 9000 years ago we are enmeshed in hazel thickets, which cover the island from end to end; the shores of inland lakes are awash with hazel-nuts. But the floruit of the hazel is short, because if we stand beside the Irish end of the land-bridge we can see the taller trees, elm, oak and pine, pushing in, and they quickly overshade the hazel. These trees react differently to different soil conditions, and we see elm flourish where the soil is limy, oak on less calcareous soils (Pl 8), and pine is especially common along the Atlantic seaboard.

We keep a sharp look-out on the shores of any small lakes we pass, hoping to see washed-up fragments of two plants that live submerged in the water. These are the naiads, widespread in temperate and tropical regions. One species, *Naias flexilis*, still grows in a few ponds along the western seaboard; common in North America, it has been thought to be a survivor from some previous warm stage in Ireland, but it is unlikely to have survived the cold conditions of 11,000 years ago. The second, *N. marina*, is now extinct in Ireland, and in Britain it survives only in the Norfolk Broads. Fossil finds show that both had a fairly wide distribution in nutrient-rich lakes in Ireland, except in the south-east, but had largely disappeared by about 4000 years ago.

32

As we move along, temperatures have been recovering steadily, and about
6500 years ago the summers are extremely pleasant. Now as we move further
on, June days are no longer as warm. The Indian Summer, or 'Climatic
Optimum' as modern workers call it, when summer temperatures were a degree
or two above present levels, is over. Are we already heading towards the next
cold stage? The drop in temperature may have helped in the extinction of *Naias
marina*. Conversely it may have assisted in the expansion of the alder, which
had first appeared about 7000 years ago.

The first human inhabitants; Larnian settlements

As we were following the trails of arriving plants and animals, we neglected the
trail of the most important immigrant, man, and must now retrace our steps to
the point of his arrival, about 9000 years ago. Thin streams of smoke draw us to
the mouth of the River Bann in north-east Antrim.

The Bann was the thoroughfare up which migratory fish, such as the salmon
and the eel, made their way to and from Lough Neagh, and at certain times of
the year there must have been enormous rushes of fish, whose capture was fairly
easy. We arrive when a movement of the eels is on, and Mesolithic hunter-
fishermen are congregated on the banks of the river. We see a village of round
tents, supported on slender rods and covered with hides of the red deer (Pl 9).
They have bows and harpoons armed with narrow rods of flint, known as
microliths, and with these they wreak havoc among the crowded eels and any
waterfowl that come their way. We also have the excitement of watching
ospreys engorging themselves. The catch is too large to be eaten immediately,
and much of the smoke is coming from a complicated arrangement of hearths
and racks, where the surplus is being smoked for future consumption or for
trading.

We only see a few other such groups, one in Co Offaly at Boora, near
Tullamore in the Shannon drainage-basin, and a third near Cappoquin,
overlooking the River Blackwater. The association with rivers is significant.

Leaving the mouth of the Bann we move upstream, and suddenly realise that
we have lost contact with the early fishermen; in fact they seem to have
vanished completely. But about one thousand years later as we approach
Newferry, at the point where the Bann flows out of Lough Neagh, more dense

masses of smoke appear. We come upon a group of people who are filleting fish prior to smoking them, and we notice that they are all using a standard triangular flint knife. Some of these may have been made on the spot, but they are more likely to have been made on the nearby Antrim coast, where supplies of flint are abundant. We move on to the Antrim coast, to Larne, where wave erosion of the chalk cliffs has left the beach rich in flint nodules, and here we find a party of flint-workers, or knappers (see 3.1).

We watch a man pick up an oval piece of flint and knock one end off it, just as we would open a boiled egg. Turning the new flat end of the core upwards he knocks flakes off the flanks of the core till he reaches the point where one further carefully directed blow detaches a flake shaped like an isosceles triangle with a ridge up its centre and two sharp edges, thus creating a double-edged knife. He may narrow the base of the triangle by further work, and may blunt at least part of one sharp edge, thus ensuring that the edge will not cut the finger of the filleter.

An experienced flint-worker, he produces a number of knives quite quickly. In the process he creates hundreds of waste flakes, and these lie around him. He is working on the sea-shore, and the next spring-tide will carry away both the

3.1. The Aborigines are using flint-working methods that were familiar to the Mesolithic people at Larne some 8000 years ago. (National Library of Australia)

35

Pl 2. (See p13) The Galty Mountains rise. About 300 million years ago, great earth pressures thrust against the south of Ireland. East-west folding lifted the rocks of Cork and Kerry as high as today's Himalayas. The Galty range was also created, but today we see only its cut-down stumps. (Bord Fáilte/Irish Tourist Board)

debris and some of the beach pebbles to a place where slackening currents will build them into an intertidal spit. Eight thousand years ago the relative movement of land and sea after the Ice Age had not yet completely stabilised. At Larne, later uplift raised the spit above sea-level, and if an archaeologist digs in the raised spit, he will find thousands of discarded flakes, but only a few completed implements. Because of the special abundance of these characteristic flakes at Larne, we call these people the Larnians.

We drift on southwards past Strangford Lough, where numerous drumlin islands provide suitable sites for Larnian settlements. And from here on, especially around the shores of Dublin Bay and as far south as Carnsore Point, Co Wexford, we are never out of sight of Larnian camp-fires. The same is true if we turn inland from Dublin and visit the Westmeath lakes.

As we follow the Larnians along, we notice some small areas where the woodlands have clearly been interfered with. Older trees have been cut down and there is a bushy growth of young scrub. Deer much prefer to graze on lush young twigs than on older branches, and are attracted to these clearances, where they can be ambushed and killed. We also see the Larnian knappers taking oval flint pebbles and turning them into rough sharp-edged felling-axes by striking off flakes around the circumference of the pebble.

About 7700 years ago we move a little distance west of Dublin to Clondalkin, where water highly charged with calcareous material is trickling away from some exposed crags of limestone. The water moves through the grass and across some small open-water ponds that contain an ecological group of pond-snails. Evaporation is taking place, and tufa (a porous, sponge-like form of calcite) is being deposited, entrapping shell and plant debris. Poking around, one of our party picks up a small piece of worked flint — Larnians have been here.

Pl 3. (See p15) About sixty-five million years ago, north-east Ireland was an inferno. Massive underground explosions, much greater than today's nuclear tests, threw molten rock and cinders high into the air. Great surface cracks allowed molten rock to escape more quietly and cover the ground with layers of basalt. All nearby life was killed. (From Eruptions of Hawaiian Volcanoes by Robert I Tilling et al. Photo by J D Griggs)

We find that such masses of tufa, all with related groups of shells, are not uncommon, and following them we drift eastwards. Suddenly we notice that the sea is not far away on both sides of us, and we realise that we are following a land-bridge, and that among the plants and animals we are passing there are newcomers making their way into Ireland. When we have already moved some little distance into Wales, where we still continue to see the same association of molluscs, we turn back lest the final severance of the land-bridge would leave us cut off from Ireland.

We tramp on through dense, tall deciduous woodland, which on the better soils is dominated by oak, elm and alder. If we rise in altitude, birch and pine

37

become more important, and the same happens if we move to the poorer soils of the west. All of a sudden, about 5000 years ago, we notice that many of the elms are dying. Our coleopterist points out that in these trees a boring beetle is at work below the bark, and that the trees that are heavily infested must die.

Ireland's first farmers; megalithic tombs; woodland declines

At the mouth of the River Boyne, we turn inland in the hope of following the Larnian folk upstream. We come upon a forest clearance where quite large trees have been felled. The still-standing stumps carry the scars of much cleaner axe-strokes than we have seen before, and while we argue about these we hear the unmistakable lowing of a domestic cow. We look at our chronometers which tell us that we are 6000 years before the present day. Ireland's first Neolithic farmers have arrived, bringing with them domestic animals and cereal crops. Their seed-stock has been only roughly winnowed, and along with the grains of corn there are seeds of many other plants — weeds if they become too numerous.

Moving cautiously on, in the area of Drogheda where Townley Hall stands today, we come to a field growing a barley crop, with at its far edge a rectangular hut built of planks. A woman sits beside a smouldering fire preparing food in a pottery vessel; it has a round bottom, but tapers in at the top to a mouth of smaller diameter, which gives it a shouldered appearance. A man near her has a polished stone axe mounted in a wooden haft by his side, but he is stripping bark and side-branches off some hazel-rods with a flake of flint that has a deep, crescentic notch on one side, known as a hollow-scraper. Beyond the hut there is pasture, in which a group of small black cows are grazing contentedly.

We continue upstream, and 4700 years ago, still in the Townley Hall area, we come to another farm where we see quite different activities in progress. Where a round hut supported by stakes had formerly stood, a structure of large stones is being erected, and we ask ourselves 'Is this destined to be a tomb, and are we for the first time seeing recognition of the ingrained human belief that after death there is a further spirit life, where homes will also be necessary?' We stand spellbound as we first see a patterned foundation laid out, within which huge stones are next erected to form a short passage, which in turn is roofed with large stones. Now a procession of elaborately dressed mourners appears, preceded by an impressive figure bearing aloft an open-mouthed, round-bottomed pottery bowl, decorated with stab-marks, which contains the cremated remains of the owner of the farm. He deposits the bowl in the passage, and then all fall to, first to define the grave with a kerb of standing-stones, and then, using wooden spades, to throw up a mound of earth over the megalithic tomb.

Continuing our slow wandering upstream, we notice that agricultural countryside is everywhere replacing woodland, and that the farms are packed more and more closely together. There are innumerable round huts, some in clusters, just as we can see in some areas of Africa today. About 4500 years ago we reach an isolated ridge, which rises between the valleys of the Boyne and the Mattock. We are stunned by the scale of the tomb-building activities around us (Pl 10). Someone has waved a magic wand over the tomb we have just passed, and not only has its mound, its kerb and its chamber been multiplied hundreds of times, but the end of the simple passage has been replaced by a large chamber off which are several smaller chambers. And this is not all: as the great stones lie waiting to be erected, craftworkers with a wooden mallet in one hand and a quartz point in the other are incising elaborate curvilinear designs of magical significance into their flanks.

All sorts of materials, including food, are required in vast quantities. For food, the local fields are doing their best — trees have virtually disappeared — but it is clear that their fertility is rapidly being exhausted. The group must be bringing in food from elsewhere — but from how far? We take ourselves to the vicinity of Ballycastle in north-west Mayo. Here the same time ago, where a gentle hill-slope runs down to a sea-cliff, we see another group of mourners around a megalithic tomb. The ceremonies they are conducting are different to those we have seen on the Boyne, but the basic underlying beliefs must be very similar. At the north-east end of this tomb the covered passage ends in an oval court delimited by large stones. As soon as the cremated remains have been deposited in the passage, large numbers of people appear who quickly bury the tomb below an oval mound of stones.

The ceremony over, we take a better look at the surrounding countryside. It is divided by stone walls into a rectangular grid of fields in which large numbers of small black cattle are grazing. The local population cannot be very numerous,

39

cont. p 42

Pl 4. (See p22) This old lake-basin near Ratoath, Co Meath, produced the remains of many tundra plants, as well as bones of Irish giant deer and reindeer. Scenes such as this could be found in many parts of Ireland during the later stages of the Ice Age. (Board Fáilte/Irish Tourist Board)

40

Pl 5. (See p28) Drumlins, Co Fermanagh. The forces that moulded these oval mounds of glacial debris are not yet clearly understood. (Joe Cornish)

Pl 6. (See p30)
11,000 years ago there
was a small ice-cap on
the Wicklow Mountains,
and ice from it filled the
Glendasan valley. The
scene was similar to this
present-day view of
Oraefajohull, Iceland.
(G F Mitchell)

Pl 7. (See p30) Glendalough, Co Wicklow. Some 11,000 years ago, Glendalough was also filled with
moving ice, which smoothed its valley sides to their present shape. (Board Fáilte/Irish Tourist Board)

41

cont. from p 39

and they are never going to eat all these cows. We take a look at the polished
stone axes these people are using; they are not all of local stone, and we
recognise two that have come from an axe factory in Co Antrim. They must be
buying axes by selling cows; but where will the cows end up? Will some of
them get as far as the Boyne? We resolve that from now on we will keep a sharp
eye out for droving-roads, along which cattle could be moved for long distances.

The arrival of the Bronze Age; spread of blanket-bog

We move on to south-west Ireland to the vicinity of Schull. Looking north we
see an isolated rocky hill, Mount Gabriel. There is so much smoke that we think
the whole mountain must be ablaze, but through our binoculars we can see that
there are many people at work among the fires. We climb the slope and mingle
with them, and immediately see that they are miners digging out copper ore.
Our chronometers say 3500 years ago, and this is our first contact with metal.
We notice that the appearance of the men — rather round-headed — is different
to that which we have grown accustomed to, there are bows whose
accompanying arrows have barbed and tanged points mounted on them, and
tucked safely in hollows in the rock there are well-made, thin-walled, decorated
pottery vessels. These are beakers, holding refreshing drinks for the thirsty
miners. The people we are looking at must be invading prospectors. The
pinewoods of the hillslope are melting away as endless fires are built against the
rockface, so that it will shatter when water is thrown against its hot surface.

We see people collecting ore-rich pieces from the broken rock, but there is
no sign of smelting; they must be doing this at some other place, where timber is
more readily available. We observe that these people also have megalithic
tombs, but again of a different pattern. The tombs are essentially stone boxes set
in a wedge-shaped cairn of stones, often on a site facing south-west and
commanding an open view. We walk down the mountain to the coast at Altar,
and see a splendid tomb perched on the edge of a low cliff (Pl 11); does this
mark the place where the miners made their landfall?

We return to the Boyne Valley as the newcomers arrive there. The great
megalithic tombs are abandoned, and only sporadic cultivation is taking place
on the wide expanses of neglected fields. The Beaker folk feel that powerful
spirits must still frequent the area. In order that their own spirits may not feel

unwelcome they decide to renew the sanctity of the site according to their own rites, which chiefly take place within circular arenas. Sometimes they define the arena by a ring of tall standing-stones, as at Stonehenge, but more commonly in Ireland by massive wooden posts. At Newgrange in Co Meath we see ceremonies taking place within the arena, which has been set up immediately beside the entrance to the great tomb. Animals are being cut open and divinations are being based on the arrangement of their entrails. There are pits within the ring, and pieces of the bodies of the sacrificed animals are being placed in these. We move a short distance to Knowth, where we see a similar, though much smaller, ring of posts with a specially arranged portal, again beside the entrance to the older tomb. Several round huts are occupied, but no ceremonies were taking place when we passed by.

The houses of the bulk of the population are scattered where low slopes look down on marshy ground, for these people know that if you want hot water in some quantity it is easier to dig a hole in wet ground and let water fill it naturally, than make a big vessel of bronze or pottery. Red-hot stones are then thrown into the water to bring it to the boil. The great numbers of these cooking-places, or *fulacht fiadh*, must mean that each household has its own fire-site (see 3.2). The sites seem to be used for water-heating only, as there are no bits of bone or broken pottery lying around. We did see one man taking a bath in the left-over hot water.

As we reach a point about 3000 years ago, we notice with increasing concern that the whole sky has become overcast by a grey cloud, whose deepening intensity cuts off a great deal of daylight. Everywhere crop yields are reduced and beasts pine, while the farmers light blazing bonfires and bang gongs in the hope of chasing away the evil spirits that have brought about the gloom. We feel that there must have been a tremendous volcanic explosion somewhere, and that suspended ash is cutting down the light. But after about twenty years of shadow the sky clears, trees flourish, and the fields resume their productivity.

After this setback the population rapidly increases, and bronze tools and weapons, which are much more efficient than those of stone, become more readily available. Technology is increasing also, and we see for the first time a man using a primitive type of plough, known as the ard. Instead of the man making separate strokes with a mattock or a spade, the ox, when fitted with

43

appropriate harness, draws a blade or share of bronze or stone mounted in a wooden frame through the surface of the field in one continuous motion. But the soil is only stirred, not turned over, and there must be cross-ploughing. We now find ourselves frequently crossing small, square fields. The trees are thinning out still further.

Pl 9. (See p34) This is the sort of fishing village we saw on the banks of the River Bann 9000 years ago. (G F Mitchell)

Pl 10. (See p39) Knowth, Co Meath. Some 4500 years ago, these minor megalithic tombs stood patiently awaiting the next ceremonial interment. (G F Mitchell)

Pl 11. (See p42) Altar, Co Cork. If we had happened to be here 3500 years ago, we might have seen a group of copper-miners from Brittany come ashore in this quiet cove, and, finding rich ore nearby, choose a site overlooking the cove to build their communal tomb. (William O'Brien)

Pl 8. (Opposite) (See p32) Oak woods, Tullamore, Co Offaly. Some 7000 years ago, our wanderings never took us far from dense woodlands like these. (Daniel L Kelly)

3.2. Ballyvourney, Co Cork. We await the return of some local Bronze Age folk, 3000 years ago, carrying with them the meat they intend to cook and wood for the fire. They will heat stones in the fire, and then drop the stones into the trough to bring the water to the boil. (M J O'Kelly)

If we leave the fertile Boyne Valley and wander westwards, we see that all is not well with the fields. Their surfaces are becoming wetter and are being invaded by patches of rushes. Soon the purple moorgrass (*Molinia caerulea*) will move in and begin to cover the ground like a blanket. During the next few hundreds of years of our wanderings we shall see this blanket-bog cover almost the whole of western Ireland — meaning for this purpose all ground lying west of a line running from Belfast Lough through Galway Bay and on to Clonakilty Bay off the Cork coast. Fierce arguments break out as to the reason for this change. Has the climate become marginally cooler and wetter in some subtle

46

way? Has chemical weathering of the soil leached iron out of the surface layers and precipitated it some centimetres down as an impermeable layer of iron pan? Have the farmers accelerated this process by tilling the surface soil, and so making it more accessible to the leaching process? On Valencia Island off the Kerry coast we watch the local farmers carefully burning strips of heath so as to encourage the growth of young shoots; does the ash from these fires wash down into the soil and lodge in the pores separating the soil particles, and so bring about impedance of drainage?

Everywhere on the lower slopes of land we see fields losing out to bog. About 3000 years ago, at Bunnyconnellon, Co Mayo, on the western slopes of the Ox Mountains, ridged arable fields are being overwhelmed by blanket-bog. We watch men with spades build up the ridges, and are fascinated to see that this type of cultivation, which has now virtually disappeared from Ireland, is widely practised. We wish we could learn what they call this operation. Later, in Early Christian times, the ridges were called 'immaire', but they subsequently declined into being wrongly called 'lazy-beds'.

At this time, about 3000 years ago, more and more deposits of ore are being worked in Europe, and bronze is being produced in greater quantities, and falling in price. There are wide trading-complexes in western Europe, and we see new types of bronze implements everywhere, purchased by the export of Irish gold ornaments. Living standards are higher, particularly in the lower Shannon basin.

Some groups are quite clearly doing better than others, and this is giving rise to regional tensions. An armaments industry springs up, as everyone wants the new-style slashing-sword, and also the shield with which to protect the body against its cuts. Now for the first time we see sentries posted round the more important houses, whose owners have, not only racks of weapons, but also valuable gold ornaments, cauldrons for special feasts, and musical instruments stored away inside.

Iron replaces bronze; Celtic influences abound; boglands under threat
We are getting still more bewildered by the ever-changing scene, when one day we pass a forge and hear a distinctive trill from the anvil. We peer inside, and sure enough the blacksmith is forging what can only be a bar of iron. We now

47

Pl 12. (See p49) Raised-bog vegetation. The bottom of the picture shows a pool filled with green Sphagnum *moss, on which red* Drosera *(sundew) is growing. A knoll of* Sphagnum *rises behind, on which are flowering, from left to right, white* Rhynochospora, *pale* Erica *(heather) and yellow* Narthecium. (G F Mitchell)

Pl 13. (See p61) Clonmacnoise, Co Offaly. Amid the ruins of the monastery, we look out on the callows beside the Shannon, and listen eagerly for the corncrake. (Bord Fáilte/Irish Tourist Board)

enter a period of further change, which circles round us like a whirlwind, as we see religion, language, weapons and art styles all alter completely. The organised chieftainships of the Celtic world of central Europe are moving into Ireland.

We see these changes taking place everywhere, and try to identify what, if any, common traits are shared by the chieftains. Their hill-forts are perhaps one. As its name implies, the hill-fort is usually on a prominence, where a circular area is defined by an outer ditch and an inner bank. Some centres are obviously strategic, others are centres for new religious practices.

We move a short distance to the west of Armagh where 2000 years ago at Emain Macha we see a low hill surrounded by a fort-like bank and ditch. A circular wooden house, 40m (130 ft) in diameter, stands inside it. But some change in ritual must be in progress, for the tribesmen are now busy carrying large stones into the interior of the house until they have it completely full. That completed, they first heap earth and sods onto the top of the house, and then set fire to the house itself, which chars away quietly. Is it just some change in ritual, or are they terrified lest their precious shrine should fall into impious hands?

Disquiet is everywhere. We move on to the vicinity of Dundalk, Co Louth, and find, straddling the route from Leinster to Ulster, a small but strong enclosure, whose oak timbers have the same age as those in the house at Emain Macha. From here we see a defensive bank and ditch running away westwards — it was obviously ploughed up by the snout of a giant wild boar, and so it is the Black Pig's Dyke. We follow the dyke westwards as it threads its way across drumlins and raised-bogs, until we emerge on the Sligo coast. As we cross the Shannon we see that a loop in the river has been turned into a strong defence point.

Watching the development of raised-bogs has been one of the joys of our trip so far. When we started out, lakes were the dominant feature of lowland country, and the calls of red-throated divers were listened to eagerly; we watched the swoops of the ospreys. Then fen, low marshy land, began to creep out from the margins and we admired the waterlilies and the bulrushes, and heard the boom of the bitterns. As the mat of fen-vegetation thickened, rainwater, constantly moving downwards, leached away any nutrient that survived, enabling bog-moss (*Sphagnum*) to establish itself (Pl 12). *Sphagnum*

49

has acidifying qualities, and it was soon joined by sedges, cotton-grass and heathers (especially ling), and a self-perpetuating specialised community was set up. Rainwater could supply all the nutrient needs of the community, whose surface started to rise towards the source of its supply, and the bog surface gradually became a gently rounded dome. As the fen margin crept out toward the centre of the lake, the bog-edge followed; when open water disappeared, bog covered the whole basin; the calls of the grouse and the blackcock replaced the booms of the bittern.

As the bog expanded, it blocked the surface drainage of landscape around. Gradually the surface became so wet that any surviving trees were killed, and fen-plants, notably the reed (*Phragmites*), invaded it and started to build up fen-peat. After the peat had reached a certain thickness, nutrient supply became blocked, rain leached the surface, and the *Sphagnum* community established itself.

We speculate that in given circumstances and without human interference there is no limit to peat expansion in Ireland, with the exception perhaps of the drier south-east corner. If our walk was to continue indefinitely, would we see dry ground restricted to an ever-narrowing belt, with expanding raised-bog within it, and down-creeping blanket-bog outside it? Would even the belt itself one day be engulfed?

As we move on westwards we have to make many detours to avoid picking our way step by step across the large raised-bogs we shall encounter. But for the first time we come across a group of people who are tackling these obstacles to travel in a determined manner. They are laying a roadway, stout enough to carry wheeled vehicles, by placing substantial oak trunks transversely across the bog surface. To lessen the chance of settlement of the road, they are throwing down a foundation of small pieces of wood and scrap timber from abandoned houses in advance of the oak trunks. The roadway is heading towards a drumlin that rises like an island above the bog surface. Earlier in our travels we have seen light trackways of hazel-rods thrown down in wet places, but this is the first piece of serious road-making we have encountered.

Sadly we appreciate that this is the initiation of continuing human attack on the Irish raised-bogs, an attack that rapidly becomes two-pronged. Raised-bogs get in the way, and can also yield immense quantities of fuel. We had already noted that these people habitually used turf rather than wood as a fuel.

We turn back towards Wicklow, but make a few detours on the way. We visit the Hill of Tara in Co Meath, which is now a very important cemetery with many graves of the barrow type — a central mound surrounded by a bank and ditch. Although the hill is fairly inconspicuous, there is a superb view from its summit. The whole surroundings are given over to farming, and trees are few in number.

We swing aside to have still another look at Knowth, where surprises await us. During most of the Bronze Age the area had subsided into oblivion, but now some Iron Age chieftain has seen the strategic possibilities of the big mound, and by opening up two great ditches around its slopes he has turned the top into a strong point. He is a cattle-king, as cattle form half the stock we see in his fields and yards, although there is also a large complement of pigs, and a smaller number of sheep. He is no isolated peasant; he gambles with dice, and the ladies in his retinue have necklets and armlets of glass, and also bronze finger-rings.

We have been to the Wicklow Mountains before, some 350 million years ago, but the landscape has dramatically changed, erosion having removed many hundreds of metres of rock. At Baltinglass, Co Wicklow, we are at a complicated border between the granite and the older rock into which it was intruded, and the older rocks have been dissected out by erosion into pinnacles at about 300m (985 ft). We are amazed to see that each pinnacle is crowned by a curved stone wall, which encloses a fort, and that the hill-slopes are divided by a further series of walls. Big numbers of sheep are grazing on the rough grass of the hill-slopes, and people are marshalling them into pens and enclosures, as it is summertime. We are amused that they have no shears, and are tugging fistfulls of wool out of the sheep's flanks. The tops of the mountains are now covered by grassy blanket-bog, and we can see many more sheep wandering there.

The early medieval period
Suddenly, about 1700 years ago, new changes begin to sweep across the countryside. We cannot see any traces of battle or defeat, but the whole layout of the countryside is transformed. New farm structures appear. Great numbers

51

of a new type of farm unit, an enclosed circular space about 30m (98 ft) in width surrounded by a bank with an external ditch, are being dotted across the grasslands, where only a few scattered trees survive here and there. Within the unit are a small house and some byres, the space itself being divided by fences into paddocks (see 3.3).

3.3. About 1200 years ago, whenever we passed through an area where the soil was clayey, we saw many of these small farm units or 'raths'. (Angela Clarke)

rath

Around the rath, as the farm unit is known, most of the land is carrying heavy herds of cattle, but there are also hedged fields in which a developed type of plough is at work. The rather blunt ard-point had worked well as long as the soil revealed by woodland clearance remained fairly open in texture. But once the soil had been bound by a dense growth of grass rootlets, the ard became less effective. Someone in the Roman world had had the bright idea of mounting a sharp knife, the coulter, on the frame of the plough in front of the ard-point, or share, and this — by cutting through the grass-roots — greatly speeded up the work of ploughing; but cross-ploughing was still necessary.

The raths appear to lie in organised clusters, and there are routeways, which will develop into roads, joining up some of the clusters.

The security provided by the bank and ditch was greatly appreciated, and in areas rich in lakes, round stockades were built where the water was shallow.

The interior was filled with earth, peat or rubbish until an artificial island, the crannog, was created (see 3.4). Inside his crannog the farmer is personally more secure, but he cannot protect his livestock, as he could in his rath.

The pagan Roman Empire, which gradually gave way to the Christian world, is now well established in Britain. As we move along we keep hoping to see a

crannog

3.4. Craggaunowen, Co Limerick. A speculative crannog builder has completed the job, and is now looking for a buyer. (Shannon Airport Development Co. Ltd)

small Roman scouting-party reconnoitring the Irish countryside, or at least see a group of people chattering in tolerable Latin, but we have to be content with examining some standing-stones with provincial transliterations of simple dedications in ogham script.

Although we see no evidence of physical Roman presence, it is clear that new ideas are once more flooding in. Some of the plots within the rath are turned into gardens, where vegetables new to Ireland — leeks, cabbages, onions and celery — are being grown, along with many new weeds.

We pass a ploughed field whose surface is laid out in ridges and furrows, and

53

realise that the plough as we know it has arrived in Ireland. Whereas the coulter had been fitted on the plough-frame in front of the share, or point, the sloping mould-board is now tucked in behind it. As the mould-board advances, it turns the sod upside down, thus burying the surface weeds and exposing the soil to be broken down by winter frost and rain. Cross-ploughing is no longer necessary.

As we move along we notice a cluster of small standing-stones, which carry an incised cross and a name written in characters adapted from the Roman alphabet. Two milestones have been passed, Christianity and literacy have reached Ireland. Houses begin to crowd round some of the cemeteries, and many of the converts take to a monastic way of life.

Rumours reach us of a large monastery, almost a town, on the banks of the Shannon at Clonmacnoise, and as there is an esker or sand-ridge nearby, with people moving backwards and forwards along it, we take that track to the west. We approach a large settlement, and see for the first time small rectangular stone buildings, the churches of the monastery. One group is using large stones to lay out a circular foundation, and we realise that a round tower is in the making.

Times of battle and unrest; plague and disease; changes in land ownership
All of a sudden a tremendous alarm breaks out and everybody starts to run, pointing upstream as they do. We turn our heads in the same direction, and see a Viking longship advancing downstream. The boat halts and a well-organised landing-party steps ashore. They first try to corral some monks against a corner of a wall, where they are quickly manacled and left in the charge of a guard. It is essential that no severe violence be used, for a slave with a broken limb is of little value. They then proceed to the churches where they strip the altars of their valuable vessels and plunder the chests around the walls of the church for clothing and weapons. They withdraw as rapidly as they appeared, frog-marching their captives to the boat. We move sadly back along the esker.

As we cross Westmeath once more, about 500 years ago, we notice a mound on a hilltop, a mound that was not there when we last passed that way. To get close to the mound we encounter a field-pattern we have not seen before, an open-field pattern of long narrow strips, a shape that will accommodate the heavy mould-board plough. The mound (or motte) has a small enclosed area at

54

its foot (the bailey). It was erected quickly to guard a seized area of land.

Now the newcomers, the Anglo-Normans — assisted by press-ganged natives — are laying out a manor for some intruding Norman knight. Some are building the mansion, others are at work on the church, the barn and the mill, in the hope of creating a little Pembrokeshire in the Irish midlands (see 3.5).

For some time we have been aware that the weather is unusually clement, and this is making things rosy for the wheat that the new farmers are growing in their long fields. In June we take a walk through the growing wheat, which to our modern eyes is a very 'dirty' crop crowded with weeds. But the sight is a beautiful one: cornflowers, poppies, corn marigolds, and corn cockle, all in full and colourful bloom. We also see some rabbits scampering round, as they have inevitably escaped from the specially built warrens into which they were introduced. There are also fallow deer in deerparks, and new fish, perch and tench, originally in fish-ponds, are escaping into the rivers.

But the climatic improvement turns out to be short-lived, and the yields from the wheat fields grow less and less. Our cloaks of invisibility not only protect us from being seen, they also protect us from infection, and so we watch safely but horror-stricken as plague decimates the undernourished peasants. The whole manorial system collapses around us.

Some 450 years ago we run into English military activity in the midlands. Soldiers are driving the local population, half-Irish, half-Norman, from the lands, and surveyors are busy dividing them up into suitable farm units. To produce an immediate cash-crop and to give more farmland, any surviving woods are being savagely attacked, to be exported as timber or barrel-staves, or burned locally to provide charcoal for iron furnaces. Immense changes are being produced in the local landscape. The unit is under the control of a favourite of the Tudor Crown, who flaunts roses and portcullises everywhere on his castle. He works the land by importing settlers from Britain, who bring new implements and new breeds of cattle and sheep with them.

We also see that the previous occupants do not take easily to their displacement; if they are to be driven off their settlements, they will not settle, but will take to the nomadic life-style of 'creaghting'. Whole communities and their livestock amble past us, camping here and there, and turning their cattle out to graze on the regenerating saplings in the devastated woods. We no longer

3.5. (Following spread) Ballyduagh, Co Tipperary. We visit a thirteenth-century Norman manor and see the house (bottom right), the church (top left), and a scatter of houses and plots. (Valerie Bell)

55

cont. p 58

cont. from p 55

hear the drumming of the woodpecker's bill, and are not really consoled when we start to see magpies instead. When summer comes we follow the nomads up to the uplands, where they camp in flimsy huts, and work almost day and night to keep up with the summer flush of milk, turning most of it into curds and butter for winter use.

Year after year we keep moving through unrest, battle or skirmish, as the Irish and English tides advance and retreat. But 300 years ago we see an English spring-tide inundate the Irish landscape, and after that Irish tides are no more than cat's-paws.

Ireland enters the 'modern' era
We watch with fascination as the Agricultural Revolution brings vast changes in its wake. The older three-field system of winter corn, spring crop and fallow vanishes, as new fenced fields provide control of stock, and manageable plots for crops, both for grazing and manuring. The turnip appears, and clover in much greater quantities than before. What had been fallow is now manured and cropped again directly. The output from the land increases hugely, and this brings increased wealth to the gentleman landlord, who has replaced the king's favourite at the top of the social pyramid. He lays out a new village or small town, where he will build houses for his labourers and a market for his produce. He decides to embellish his own demesne, putting a high wall around his property, and building a large and handsome mansion inside it. Then he turns to landscaping. For the first time we see the beech, fir and spruce growing in Ireland, and they are the heralds of many additions to the Irish flora. Aided by government grants, the gentry also begin some planting on a commercial scale, and we see the first steps being taken in the long haul to bring back to Ireland at least some element of tree-cover.

Another much more humble-looking newcomer, the potato, begins to force itself on our notice. Coming from highland in South America, this plant finds conditions in Ireland amenable, and grows and crops freely. Until about 1815 the area covered by potato fields expands slowly. The countryside is prosperous, prices in the markets are good, and the loom-rooms in the cottages are busy, where the wives and the older children are bringing in some cash by turning flax into coarse linen. Children are increasing in number, for their labour is valuable.

After the end of the Napoleonic wars we see standards fall everywhere, and real depression hits the countryside. Food prices drop away disastrously, and the opening of powered spinning mills in Belfast takes away the other source of cash.

3.6. Ballinloughane, Co Limerick. In 1850 we saw far too many of these hovels dotted down the hillsides. (K Danaher)

But there is still more marginal land further up the hillslopes to be reclaimed, and the lazy-beds and their accompanying turf cabins creep on and up (see 3.6). A crippling amount of labour is necessary, and more and more children spring up to fulfil this need. A form of desert begins to surround us; anywhere the potato can grow is under the spade, anywhere the potato cannot grow is stripped of all its woody tissue for fuel, any animal that can be trapped is eaten. Potatoes and occasional scraps of pork are the only foodstuffs, and malnutrition is everywhere. A botanical tragedy, the arrival of blight, a fungal disease, and the consequent destruction of the potato crop was all that was needed to bring about national ruin.

Astounded we look to the demesnes of the gentry, which rise like coral islands from a Sargasso Sea that is awash with destitution of man, plant and *59* animal. The surrounding atoll reef is the demesne wall with its ring of stately trees inside, the lagoon is the fields, and the volcanic core is the mansion (see 3.7) and its surrounding gardens full of exotic shrubs from America and China. Even today the demesnes can be identified by their large redwoods and firs, so different to the very much smaller trees that are re-appearing in the Irish countryside.

3.7. Mount Ievers, Co Clare. This Georgian demesne on the banks of the Shannon was at its best when we visited it in 1750. (Hugh Doran)

Moving through the later nineteenth century, when European standards rose steadily, we see some natural breath return to the Irish landscape, though it is now cut up by a network of roads and minor railway lines. No part of the country remains gravely isolated. Organisation improves, partly through government intervention and partly due to co-operative organisations. But the basic field patterns of the island remain unchanged, just as the horse (which has ousted the ox) remains the main source of traction on the farm.

But as we move through the final forty years to the present day, everything around us is in turmoil. Just as the Battle of Waterloo in 1815 brought immense changes, after VE Day in 1945 the plough-horse and the clumsy implements he drags along disappear, as the tractor and its hydraulically controlled attachments sweep across the countryside. There is no longer any control on field-size, and many miles of hedgerow which were happy hosts to plants and birds are swept away. In 1973 the whole Irish landscape was dragged into the EC net. Plans drawn on a European scale cannot be honed down to fit the infinite small-scale variation of the Irish landscape. New practices meet our eyes at every turn; stocky continental breeds replace the traditional half-bred cow; on better soils new races of cereals are intensively cultivated; maize appears in sunnier areas; great blocks of conifers spread over poorer land. Are we watching the final demise of the small farmer? Is he to turn into a mini-hotelier? If he quits, who will 'garden' the landscape? Who will 'garden' the vast areas of 'cutaway' that have followed on the wholesale removal of peat?

Our journey ends, on a sunny May morning, 1994, on a bank beside a callow on the Shannon at Clonmacnoise (Pl 13), where we listen to the corncrake and regard his perilous status in the Irish countryside as a symbol of the changes that are constantly transforming it. To say what it will look like one hundred years on, we leave to others.

BIBLIOGRAPHY

Edwards, K J and Warren, W (eds). 1985. *The Quaternary History of Ireland.* Academic Press, London

Holland, C H (ed). 1981. *A Geological History of Ireland.* Scottish Academic Press, Edinburgh

Mitchell, Frank. 1986, 1990. *Shell Guide to Reading the Irish Landscape.* Country House, Dublin

Ryan, Michael (ed). 1991. *The Illustrated Archaeology of Ireland.* Country House, Dublin